Hal•Leonard
Easy **INSTRUMENTAL PLAY-ALONG**

 Audio Access Included

CHRISTMAS CAROLS
FOR **ALTO SAX**

T0070928

CONTENTS

To access audio visit:
www.halleonard.com/mylibrary

Enter Code
2925-6817-2612-6939

Audio Arrangements by Peter Deneff
Tracking, mixing, and mastering by BeatHouse Music

ISBN 978-1-4803-9602-9

HAL•LEONARD®
CORPORATION
7777 W. BLUEMOUND RD. P.O. BOX 13819 MILWAUKEE, WI 53213

In Australia Contact:
Hal Leonard Australia Pty. Ltd.
4 Lentara Court
Cheltenham, Victoria, 3192 Australia
Email: ausadmin@halleonard.com.au

Visit Hal Leonard Online at
www.halleonard.com

2

ANGELS WE HAVE HEARD ON HIGH

Traditional French Carol

CHRIST WAS BORN ON CHRISTMAS DAY

Traditional

Play 3 times

COME, ALL YE SHEPHERDS

Traditional Czech Text
Traditional Moravian Melody

COME, THOU LONG-EXPECTED JESUS

Words by CHARLES WESLEY
Music by ROWLAND HUGH PRICHARD

GOOD CHRISTIAN MEN, REJOICE

14th Century Latin Text
14th Century German Melody

JINGLE BELLS

Words and Music by
J. PIERPONT

ON CHRISTMAS NIGHT

Sussex Carol

UP ON THE HOUSETOP

Words and Music by
B.R. HANBY

JOLLY OLD ST. NICHOLAS

Traditional 19th Century American Carol

LO, HOW A ROSE E'ER BLOOMING

15th Century German Carol